EYEWITNESS DISASTER

HURRICANES!

ANGELA ROYSTON

Marshall Cavendish
Benchmark

New York

This edition first published in 2011 in the United States of America
by MARSHALL CAVENDISH BENCHMARK
An imprint of Marshall Cavendish Corporation

Other Marshall Cavendish Offices:
Marshall Cavendish International (Asia) Private Limited, 1 New Industrial Road, Singapore 536196 • Marshall Cavendish International (Thailand) Co Ltd. 253 Asoke, 12th Flr, Sukhumvit 21 Road, Klongtoey Nua, Wattana, Bangkok 10110, Thailand • Marshall Cavendish (Malaysia) Sdn Bhd, Times Subang, Lot 46, Subang Hi-Tech Industrial Park, Batu Tiga, 40000 Shah Alam, Selangor Darul Ehsan, Malaysia

Marshall Cavendish is a trademark of Times Publishing Limited

Planned and produced by Discovery Books Ltd., 2 College Street, Ludlow, Shropshire, SY8 1AN www.discoverybooks.net
Managing editor: Rachel Tisdale
Editor: Jenny Vaughan
Designer: sprout.uk.com Limited
Illustrator: Stefan Chabluk
Picture researcher: Tom Humphrey

Photo acknowledgments: Corbis: 5 (Henry Romero/Reuters), 9 (John H Clark), 11 (Dennis M Sabangan/epa), 12 (CJ Gunther/epa), 13 (Marc Serota/Reuters), 15 (Henry Romero/Reuters), 19 (Petrina Berry/epa), 27 (Gideon Mendel). FEMA: 24 (Robert Kaufmann), 29 (Bob Epstein). Getty Images: 10 (Susan Greenwood), 14 (Adalberto Roque/AFP), 16 (Mark Lewis), 21 (Mehdi Fedouach/AFP), 22 (AFP), 23 (Sam Yeh), 28 (Chris Graythen). NASA: Cover, 7. NOAA: 26. Shutterstock: 18 (Alex Neauville). US Navy: 20, 25 (DoD photo by Petty Officer 3rd Class William S Parker). Wikimedia: 17 (Infrogmation).
Cover Picture: Hurrican Rita.

Library of Congress Cataloging-in-Publication Data

Royston, Angela.
  Hurricanes / by Angela Royston.
     p. cm. -- (Eyewitness disaster)
  Includes bibliographical references and index.
  ISBN 978-1-60870-003-5
  1. Hurricanes--Juvenile literature. I. Title.
  QC944.2.R689 2011
  551.55'2--dc22
                                    2010001800

Printed in China

CONTENTS

Words in **bold** or <u>underlined</u> are defined in the Glossary on page 30.

WHAT IS A HURRICANE?

A hurricane is a severe storm. It brings winds of more than 74 miles per hour (119 kilometers per hour), heavy rain, and, often, thunder and lightning. The scientific name for a hurricane is a **tropical cyclone**. The map shows where the different names for these storms—hurricanes, cyclones, and typhoons—are used around the world.

A hurricane can last for several days. The wind becomes stronger and stronger until the center of the hurricane, called the **eye**, is overhead. The wind then suddenly drops, because the eye is calm with the strong winds swirling around it. As soon as the eye has passed on, the strong winds and heavy rains begin again.

Damage

Hurricanes can cause huge amounts of damage. They break windows and rip off roofs. They uproot trees and can destroy houses. Severe hurricanes can kill hundreds

This map shows where hurricanes, typhoons, and cyclones are most common, and the different times of the year they happen. They form over oceans and then move in the directions shown by the arrows, slowing down after they reach land.

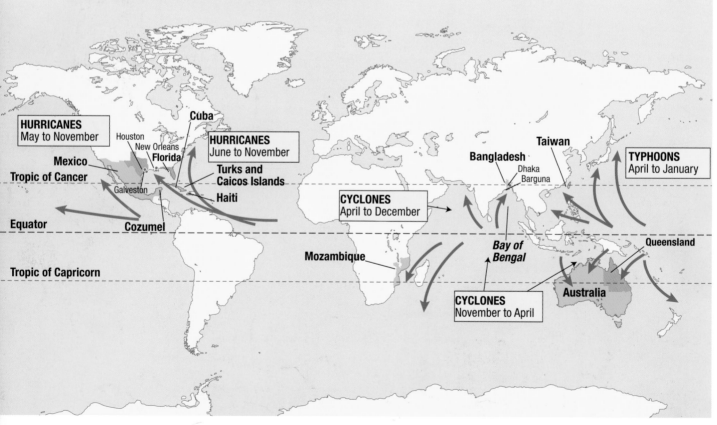

HURRICANES
May to November

Houston
New Orleans
Florida
Galveston

Cuba

HURRICANES
June to November

Turks and Caicos Islands

Haiti

Mexico

Tropic of Cancer

Cozumel

Equator

Tropic of Capricorn

CYCLONES
April to December

Mozambique

Bangladesh
Dhaka
Barguna

Taiwan

TYPHOONS
April to January

Bay of Bengal

CYCLONES
November to April

Australia

Queensland

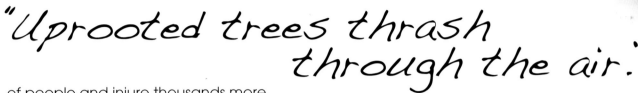
"Uprooted trees thrash through the air."

of people and injure thousands more. Even places that are not hit by the strongest part of the storm may be badly damaged.

MOZAMBIQUE MARCH 8–9, 2008

NAMING HURRICANES

Each year hurricanes are named from an alphabetical list of girls' and boys' names. If a hurricane is particularly severe or damaging, its name is dropped from the list and never used again. Different lists are used for cyclones and typhoons.

Linette Ruys was working in Cabaceira Grande, a town on the coast of the African country of Mozambique, when it was hit by the tail end of Cyclone Jokwe.

" Linette wrote:

"A colossal pounding wakes me. An **electric storm** illuminates my bedroom and instantly I am wide awake. The wind and rain are so fierce that it seems like buckets of water are being thrown through my sheeted bedroom window. Uprooted trees thrash through the air, sending palm leaves and branches flying." "

Hurricanes blow over lampposts and bring down power lines, while heavy rain causes floods.

HOW DOES A HURRICANE FORM?

A hurricane forms over warm tropical oceans, about 620 miles (1,000 km) north or south of the equator. It begins as a tropical storm, which moves across the ocean. If it crosses an area where warm, damp air is rising, the rising air creates more wind, making the storm stronger. The winds begin to spiral upward.

The arrows show the direction of the wind in different parts of a hurricane. Earth's rotation makes the winds in the eyewall spiral around the eye: counterclockwise north of the equator (shown), and clockwise south of the equator.

When the winds are constantly blowing at more than 74 miles per hour (119 kph), the storm is officially classified as a hurricane. This is when the calm eye in the center of the storm develops.

The Eye

The strongest winds are directly around the eye, in thick clouds called the **eyewall**. The eyewall also produces the heaviest rain and the most violent thunderstorms.

An average hurricane measures about 310 miles (500 km) across, but hurricanes

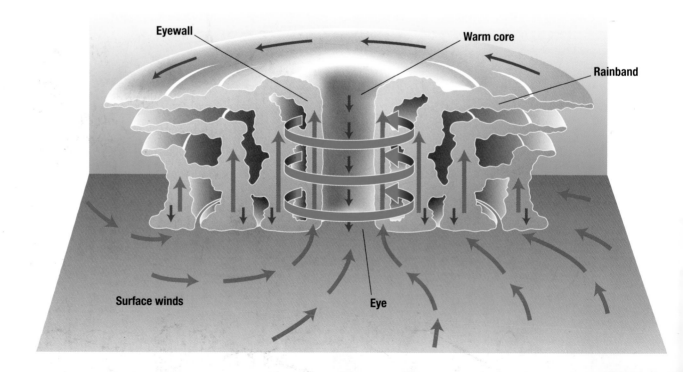

Eyewall

Warm core

Rainband

Surface winds

Eye

can be much larger or smaller. The winds and rain become less severe the further they are from the eyewall.

A hurricane moves across the ocean until it hits land. When this happens, it quickly loses its strength.

Danger to Aircraft

Hurricanes create huge clouds with strong **upwinds**. They tower high into the sky and are dangerous for aircraft. Pilots of passenger aircraft use their **radar** to look out for hurricanes and to fly around them.

"[The eye is] an amazing sight to see; it's almost like being in the center of a football stadium where the seats surrounding you are made out of clouds. At the same time, you look above ... you can see the bluest color of sky, and if you look below, you see the ocean _roiling_ with huge waves crashing."

Shirley Murillo, a hurricane expert with the National Oceanic and Atmospheric Administration (NOAA) describes the eye of a hurricane. She studies hurricanes by flying into them in a special plane.

The air inside the eye of a hurricane is calm, but the clouds around it are moving fast.

TRACKING A HURRICANE

Hurricanes are dangerous at sea, in the air, and on land. People need to know when a hurricane is coming their way. **Meteorologists** study the weather and predict how it might change. Around the world meteorologists watch out for and track developing storms. They try to predict where and when a storm will hit land.

Weather satellites orbit Earth. They transmit photographs from space of the clouds below. These photographs are the most useful way of seeing when and where a storm is brewing. As the storm moves closer to land, meteorologists then use radar to track the storm from minute to minute.

"There's a certain amount of uncertainty with storms."

Craig Fugate, Florida state emergency management director, explaining how difficult it was to predict the force of Hurricane Frances in September 2004.

Unpredictable

Some meteorologists fly special aircraft right into the eye of a hurricane. This gives them accurate measurements that tell them how strong the hurricane is.

A hurricane becomes stronger when it moves over warm water, and it weakens when it moves over land. It can also suddenly change direction. This makes it very difficult to predict exactly where a hurricane will hit land and how strong it will be when it does.

This map of the eastern United States shows the path of Hurricane Frances in 2004. The hurricane strengthened to category 4, but weakened to category 2 before it hit Florida. It then quickly lost strength as it moved over the mainland.

11 a.m. Thu. Sep. 9

N

11 p.m. Wed. Sep. 8

Atlantic Ocean

11 a.m. Wed. Sep. 8

11 p.m. Tue. Sep. 7

300 miles

11 a.m. Tue. Sep. 7

300 km

11 p.m. Mon. Sep. 6

11 a.m. Mon. Sep. 6

11 a.m. Fri. Sep. 3

11 p.m. Sun. Sep. 5

11 a.m. Sun. Sep. 5

11 p.m. Thu. Sep. 2

11 a.m. Sat. Sep. 4

This Hercules plane is one of the aircraft that researchers use to study hurricanes.

SAFFIR-SIMPSON HURRICANE WIND SCALE

Hurricanes are categorized according to the speed of their winds. A hurricane can change categories several times as the wind speeds up and slows down.

CATEGORY	WIND SPEED (mph)	DAMAGE
1 Weak	**74–95** (119–153 kph)	Some damage to mobile homes and signs
2 Moderate	**96–110** (154–177 kph)	Some damage to roofs; considerable damage to mobile homes, trees and power lines
3 Strong	**111–130** (178–209 kph)	Roofs damaged; mobile homes destroyed; roads blocked by uprooted trees; power lines down
4 Very strong	**131–155** (210–249 kph)	Roofs and walls of some buildings destroyed; nearly all trees uprooted
5 Catastrophic	**over 155** (249 kph)	Large buildings badly damaged; smaller buildings blown away

STORM WATCH

When a hurricane, cyclone, or typhoon develops, meteorologists issue warnings on radio, television, and the Internet, so people have time to prepare. There are usually two levels of warning—a storm watch and a storm warning. In Australia, for example, the Bureau of Meteorology issues a cyclone watch when a cyclone is expected within the next 48 hours. This changes to a cyclone warning when the storm is expected within the next 24 hours.

Although the weather looks calm, these two flags flying in Florida warn that a hurricane is on its way!

Hurricane on the Way!

As a hurricane approaches the Caribbean Sea or the Gulf of Mexico, the National Hurricane Center in Miami, Florida, issues a hurricane watch. This tells ships and people on land where the hurricane is, how strong it is, and the path it seems to be taking.

In and around Hong Kong, all television stations issue a series of warnings when a typhoon is expected. These warnings go from T1, which means that a typhoon is a few days away, to T10, which means that the eye of the typhoon is about to hit the island.

People camp out in a public shelter in the Philippines during the particularly severe 2009 typhoon season.

Helping Hands

Local authorities have usually planned ahead and are ready to cope when a hurricane or cyclone watch is issued. They advise people to evacuate if necessary and prepare shelters inland for people to go to during the storm.

Preparing for the Storm

Wherever hurricanes are likely, people know they must listen for warnings. In the United States people pay close attention to the Internet and keep their radios and televisions on, in case the hurricane watch becomes a hurricane warning. They also start to prepare.

It is important for anyone living in an area where hurricanes are a risk to have a plan of action in case it happens. This plan should include a place to go if they have to leave the area. People should also have a list of the essential things they will need if they decide to stay where they are.

HURRICANE WARNING!

As the hurricane or cyclone gets nearer, meteorologists issue a hurricane or cyclone warning. By this time they have a better idea of where the hurricane will hit.

When a hurricane gets close to the coast, the traffic on roads is often very heavy as people evacuate the danger area.

BE PREPARED!

Here are the steps people should take as a storm approaches:

- Board up windows

- Bring patio furniture and other loose items inside

- Buy enough food, water, medicine, and other essentials to last several days

- Bring food, water, a radio, books, and games into the safest room in the house

"It was a strange feeling."

HOUSTON, TEXAS SEPTEMBER 2005

Finding Shelter

Local authorities may order people in some areas to evacuate (leave their homes). People then either drive inland away from the storm, or they go to **evacuation centers**. Those who stay at home should shelter in the safest room—that is the room furthest from the outside walls.

> Boarding up windows protects them from being smashed by the winds. People need to make their houses and businesses as secure as possible before a hurricane hits.

Gina Carroll and her husband lived near Houston, Texas, during Hurricane Rita. Gina described how they prepared for it:

"It was a strange feeling to be staying put while others were making a vast and hurried **exodus** . . .

But here we were—him boarding up the windows and me moving furniture to the second floor; him, standing in the three-hour line at Home Depot for a **generator**, and me waiting . . . at the grocery store for . . . cases of water.

. . . Jon worked tirelessly . . . he came up with more and increasingly creative ways to secure home and family. . . .

Fortunately for us and all of Houston, we missed the **brunt** of the storm as it veered to the Northeast."

"It is like a freight train."

COZUMEL, MEXICO OCTOBER 20–21, 2005

Tony and Encarna stayed in their home on Cozumel, an island off the coast of Mexico, during Hurricane Wilma. This is part of Tony's account:

"Nine hours till Wilma. . . .

There is no one on the street. . . .

I won't be going out again tonight. . . . Wind is blasting and we just heard a big bang outside. It has begun. . . . When the gusts come it is like a freight train is rolling down the street. We keep hearing things crash outside.

Still 5 hours away from full gale. The power just went out. . . . With all the wind and heavy rain we did get a great deal of water coming in the windows and under the doors. This meant we were almost constantly mopping. . . . Friday afternoon. At 3:30 p.m. we had a 30-minute break in the action. Then . . . it went back into full force gale and rain again."

Hurricane Wilma

Hurricane Wilma reached its peak with winds of 175 miles per hour (282 kph) on October 19, two days before the eye of the storm hit Mexico. It battered the coast of Mexico for two days before it curved round and headed toward Florida. By the time it reached Florida, it had weakened from a category 5 to a category 3 hurricane.

Hurricane Wilma was the most severe hurricane ever recorded in the Caribbean Sea.

Hurricane Wilma killed at least 63 people, mostly in Haiti and Florida. It caused devastating damage, including **mudslides** in Haiti and flooding in Cuba, Mexico, and Florida. In Mexico, 23 inches (59 centimeters) of rain fell in several places.

Hurricane Wilma's fierce winds damaged buildings, filled the streets with debris, and brought down power lines. Here, on Cozumel, a marine guards against looters.

HUGE WAVES

The fierce winds of a hurricane whip up huge waves. Ships' crews listen for storm warnings and try to find a bay or harbor where they can shelter from the storm. When the waves hit the shore, they can crash over sea walls and flood the land.

Storm Surge

As the air in the center of a hurricane rises, the sea below it bulges upward. This bulge is called a **storm surge** and it can raise the level of the sea by up to 20 feet (6 meters). When the surge reaches land, the extra water sweeps up the beach and flows over the sea walls onto the land, causing flooding. In cities, the sea floods streets and buildings near the shore. In the countryside, it covers fields and **plantations**. The salt water destroys the plants and damages the soil.

AMAZING ESCAPE

Lucky to Survive

When Cyclone Sidr hit the small island of Maiher Char, Bangladesh, the islanders had nowhere to shelter. Zabbar Mia, however, managed to tie his two cousins, aged thirteen and five, to a palm tree. This saved them from the 20-foot (6-meter) wave that swept across the island. A fifth of the islanders died. "These two children are lucky to survive," said one man, who lost his wife and two sons.

Huge waves hit the shore in Baja California, Mexico, during Hurricane Ignacio in 2003. Palm trees bend in the wind and are less likely to be uprooted than other trees.

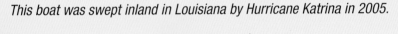
This boat was swept inland in Louisiana by Hurricane Katrina in 2005.

Helping Hands

On March 9, 2009, a huge wave whipped up by Cyclone Hamish washed fisherman James Palmer into the sea off the east coast of Australia. Luckily, he grabbed an **emergency radio beacon** that was sweeping past him. Signals from the beacon told the Central Queensland rescue services where James was. An aircraft dropped him a life raft and then, later that day, a helicopter winched him to safety.

After James was rescued, helicopter crewman Darren Bobin told the Australian press: "He was incredibly lucky. By the time we got to him the swell was up to three meters [10 feet] but he would have gone through much bigger seas than that while he was drifting."

FLOODING

Hurricanes bring heavy rain, and with the rain comes flooding. The worst flooding, however, is usually the result of storm surges. Tides, or the daily rise and fall of the sea, can make flooding worse. A storm surge at high tide causes most flooding.

New Orleans

On August 29, 2005, 80 percent of New Orleans was flooded following Hurricane Katrina. This was not caused directly by the hurricane. New Orleans lies next to Lake Pontchartrain and has **levees** (walls) to protect the city from the water. These levees had been poorly maintained. When the storm surge swept into the lake, the levees burst in 53 places.

Devastating flooding in New Orleans in 2005 caused more than 1,000 deaths.

"I've never seen water like this."

NORTH QUEENSLAND, AUSTRALIA FEBRUARY 3–4, 2009

Cyclone Ellie was only category 1 when it hit land, but its heavy rain caused widespread flooding—especially in northeastern Australia.

David Grant from the Tropical Cyclone Warning Centre said that 11 inches (282 millimeters) of rain fell on Ingham in Queensland.

Ingham resident Brooke Baskin said parts of the town that had never before flooded were being **sandbagged** as the main street went under water. "People are moving furniture upstairs and shops have been inundated," she said. The main highway north and south of the town was flooded, so that it could be reached only by boat or helicopter.

In nearby Townsville, a local resident said, "I've never seen water like this, and I've been here for 68 years."

Heavy Rain

Heavy rain swells rivers and may cause them to overflow. In towns and cities there may be more rainwater than the drains can take, so the extra water floods the streets and flows back into the buildings. This problem is made worse when the drains become blocked with leaves, branches, and other debris from the storm.

This tree-lined road in North Queensland flooded during Cyclone Ellie, when 16 inches (400 mm) of rain fell in some places.

ROAD SUBJECT TO
FLOODING
INDICATORS SHOW DEPTH

"I have lost everything."

BARGUNA DISTRICT, BANGLADESH NOVEMBER 17, 2007

In November 2007, the entire coast of Bangladesh was badly damaged by Cyclone Sidr. The cyclone devastated cities, towns and villages along the coast.

"I have lost everything," said 80-year-old Azahar Ali. He was huddled with his family, reading the Koran, when the cyclone roared in from the sea. The winds blew out the windows and ripped off the roof. Then the sea rushed in, washing the family away. Azahar Ali woke up in a **rice paddy field** to find his son and the rest of his family dead.

Dhalan Mridha, a farm worker, recalled, "Just before midnight the winds came like hundreds of demons. Our small hut was swept away like a piece of paper, and we all ran for shelter."

Cyclone Sidr

Sidr flattened homes, and schools were blown away. Barguna was one of the worst-hit places. The storm surge there was more than 16 feet (5 m) high. It flooded farmland, villages, and cities. Dhaka, the capital of Bangladesh, is about 125 miles (200 km) from the coast, but it was affected by the cyclone, too. Power lines were blown down and buildings were damaged by the wind and by flooding.

Many of the people affected by Cyclone Sidr were very poor. Their homes were made mostly of corrugated iron and were easily blown over.

This family survived the cyclone, but they had no food, clean water or shelter. Here, the children's father is trying to build a temporary shelter for them.

"Sidr is still hunting us. This is the first time in three days that I'm able to sit in front of [my] computer because of <u>power cuts</u>. Most of my relatives are living in Patukhali. They experienced a terrible storm which uprooted most of the trees, ruined the paddy fields, and damaged their homes."

Solaiman Palash in Dhaka, Bangladesh, two days after the storm.

Used to Flooding

The people of Bangladesh are used to flooding. Two mighty rivers, the Ganges and the Brahmaputra, flow across the country. Many farmers and fishermen live on the land around the mouths of these rivers. The land often floods when the rivers are full, and the people are prepared for this.

However, Sidr was unusually severe. In such a poor country, the devastation was especially hard to deal with. Few people had the funds to repair their homes, or replace damaged goods and food supplies.

MOBILIZING HELP

When a disaster occurs, many people want to help those affected. Family members who live elsewhere may send clothes and money to their relatives who have lost everything. Organizations, such as charities, and local authorities rush to help. If the disaster is very severe, the national government steps in to organize all the help that is being offered.

When roads are blocked, helicopters are often the only way of reaching people.

Helping Hands

A number of charities, such as the International Federation of Red Cross and Red Crescent Societies (IFRC), specialize in helping people after severe storms and other disasters. They can immediately send food, water, blankets, and other essential items to wherever they are needed in the world. Once the extent of the damage is known, the IFRC may give money to the national government to help to pay for repairs, too. The governments of other countries also offer money.

Assessing the Damage

First of all, the local or national government has to find out which places are most affected and what kind of help is most needed. They set up a special center to **coordinate** the help offered. The first people to reach the disaster area are often the local emergency services, such as

> "The mountain here is shaking, it is going to collapse....
> This has never happened before."

A villager quoted in the Taipei Times *on August 15, 2009, asking why rescue teams had neglected their villages.*

ambulance and fire crews, and the police. Those in charge of the **relief operation** may also call in the **armed forces** to help.

Typhoon Morakot brought with it severe mudslides, such as this one, which buried homes after torrential rain.

Help from Governments

It is mostly up to the governments of the countries hit by hurricanes to provide help to victims. For example, when Typhoon Morakot hit Taiwan on August 7, 2009, more than 10 feet (3 meters) of rain fell in some places. This caused mudslides in the mountains, which buried some villages and cut off many others. Taiwan's government sent 4,000 soldiers to help with the rescue mission. The government also appealed to other countries to send helicopters to reach people in remote areas.

By August 14, dozens of helicopters were flying over the mountains, rescuing sick and injured survivors. The helicopters also dropped food and water to thousands of trapped villagers.

EMERGENCY AID

A hurricane leaves a trail of destroyed buildings, flooded land, and shocked and frightened people. People may be killed when buildings collapse or they may be swept away and drowned by waves or floodwater. Those who survive are desperate to find out if their loved ones are safe.

Immediate Needs

The first things that hurricane survivors need are food, clean water, blankets, and shelter, such as tents. They may also need medicine. Aid workers try to get these necessities to them as quickly as possible. Aid workers particularly try to help children and injured people.

Getting into the area can be difficult because the storm may have swept away

Houses on Galveston Island, Texas, were flattened by Hurricane Ike in 2008.

"Eight newborns, all carried by their brothers or sisters."

BARGUNA DISTRICT, BANGLADESH NOVEMBER 25, 2007

roads and bridges. In September 2008, Hurricane Ike hit the island of Galveston, off the coast of Texas. So many of the buildings were destroyed that helicopters that had come to pick up survivors had trouble finding places to land.

Health Risks

Many serious diseases are carried in dirty water. When the supply of clean water is turned off or **polluted** with **sewage**, there is a risk that hurricane survivors will catch these diseases.

Eight days after Cyclone Sidr hit Bangladesh, Dr Kayvan Bozorgmehr visited a camp for 200 homeless children. He wrote:

"Lots of children had walked many kilometers to reach the [camp]. I remembered a scene from Bodma, a fishing village . . . a 4 year aged child with a spoon in his small hands scratching out a green coconut and feeding the last bits of the precious coconut-flesh to his crying brother. . . . Among 200 children there were only eight newborns, all carried by their brothers or sisters—parents or mothers were not allowed to stay in the camp."

U.S. Marines distribute clean water to victims of Cyclone Sidr.

"We need to pitch in and work together."

TURKS AND CAICOS ISLANDS SEPTEMBER 2008

On September 7, 2008, the eye of Hurricane Ike, a category 4 hurricane, hit the Turks and Caicos Islands in the Caribbean.

> Roland Hull, a **volunteer** for the British Red Cross, lives on Grand Turk, the main island. Five days after the island was struck by Hurricane Ike, he told his story to the BBC.
>
> "I'm really upset to see the state [the island's] in now. We need to pitch in and work together . . . we can make it work because that's what we do."

Hurricane Ike

Hurricane Ike brought winds of 135 miles per hour (217 kph), damaging 95 percent of the buildings on South Caicos and on Grand Turk. Medical centers were too badly hit to treat people, and stores and houses were destroyed.

Ike then headed toward Cuba, where it caused widespread flooding. A million people had been evacuated. It finally hit Galveston, Texas, on September 13 before moving inland.

Hurricane Ike also caused flooding in Haiti. It was the fourth hurricane to hit the

Damage caused by Hurricane Ike in the southern United States.

Helping Hands

People working to help after a hurricane need to concentrate on getting food and shelter to as many people as possible. This is an example of a list made by a charity worker on the island of Provo in the Caribbean after Hurricane Ike:

• expecting delivery of 160 ShelterBox temporary homes

• coordinating the receipt of 5 containers of food and water

• continuing to collect money locally and internationally

• arranging to assist with the removal and clearing of trees

• coordinating the creation and distribution of hygiene kits.

country in three weeks. This made it particularly difficult for aid agencies to reach the residents, who became more and more desperate for help.

A street in Goniaves, Haiti, after Hurricanes Ike and Hanna hit in 2008. People wade through muddy water left behind after flooding.

REPAIRING AND REBUILDING

Work on rebuilding and repairing schools, bridges, roads, and airports starts soon after a hurricane has passed. Rebuilding homes often takes much longer. Four years after Hurricane Andrew hit south Florida in 1992, some people were still living in sheds, trailers, and damaged homes. Many other people just abandoned their homes and never returned.

Wherever possible, people try to rebuild more strongly so that another hurricane will do less damage. Rebuilding, however, costs vast amounts of money. Estimates for rebuilding the levees in New Orleans, for example, were around $10 billion.

Paying the Cost

Poor countries rely on money given to them by other countries and by international organizations. Whenever there is a disaster, millions of ordinary people around the world donate money to help

After Hurricane Katrina, the city authorities were eager to show the world that life in New Orleans was returning to normal. The city has held its annual Mardi Gras parade through the streets every year since the hurricane.

Helping Hands

After Cyclone Nargis hit Burma in April 2009, the country's **military government** refused to let many aid workers into the country to help the victims. Instead about 40 percent of the aid money reached Burma **unofficially**. Some of it was passed into the country by Buddhist monks, who have monasteries in both Burma and neighboring Thailand.

"We had no roof."

HOMESTEAD, FLORIDA AUGUST 24, 1992

the survivors, too. They usually give the money to the Red Cross and other charities. Without this help, it would take even longer for survivors to rebuild their lives.

Aid workers for the American Red Cross hand out supplies to people in Florida whose towns were hit by Hurricane Andrew.

On August 24, 1992, Hurricane Andrew ripped through Homestead, Florida. Ten years later, residents had still not recovered.

In 1992, Hurricane Andrew destroyed Dan Sanabria's whole house. He describes the sound of the hurricane as:

"Something horrendous. That sound is one thing I'll never forget. . . . When the eye passed over I went out for a look and we had no roof. Three minutes after we left the bathroom, the ceiling collapsed."

Ten years later, whenever he walked along the street, he looked for good places to shelter. If he saw such a place, he thought, "That would be a good place to hide."

GLOSSARY

armed forces The army, navy, and air force.

brunt The strongest part.

coordinate Organize things to work together.

emergency radio beacon A device that sends out radio signals to alert the emergency services that someone needs help.

evacuation centers Buildings where people who have had to leave an area can stay until it is safe to return home.

exodus When a large number of people leave together.

eye (of a storm) The calm area in the center of a hurricane, cyclone, or typhoon.

eyewall The area of thick clouds, heavy rain, and strong wind that surrounds the eye of a storm.

generator A machine that makes electricity.

levees Banks along a lake or river that are built to prevent flooding.

local authorities The organizations, such as the police, responsible for local services.

meteorologists Scientists who study the weather and produce weather forecasts.

military government A government run by military officers.

mudslides Masses of mud that slide down a hillside.

plantations Large farms that grow crops, such as sugar, coffee, or rubber, to sell.

polluted Made dirty and unhealthy.

power cuts When the supply of electricity is stopped.

radar A device that detects things using radio waves and shows them on a screen.

relief operation The actions taken to bring help to people in need.

rice paddy field A field in which rice is grown.

roiling Stirred up by large waves or fast currents.

sandbagged Protected from flooding by temporary walls of bags of sand.

sewage Waste matter usually carried away in sewers.

storm surge The raised water level of the sea due to a hurricane, typhoon, or cyclone.

tropical cyclone A severe storm that includes heavy rain and high winds that spiral around a calm center.

unofficially Not approved by the authorities.

upwinds Winds that blow upward from the surface of Earth.

volunteer Someone who chooses to work without pay.

weather satellites Unmanned spacecraft that circle Earth, sending back information to meteorologists.

FURTHER INFORMATION

Books

Birch, Robin. *Extreme Weather.* Weather and Climate. New York: Marshall Cavendish Benchmark, 2010.

Chambers, Catherine. *Hurricanes.* Wild Weather. Chicago: Heinemann, 2007.

Levy, Janey. *World's Worst Hurricanes.* Deadly Disasters. New York: Rosen, 2009.

Woods, Michael and Mary B. *Hurricanes.* Disasters Up Close. Minneapolis, MN: Lerner, 2007.

Websites

www.fema.gov/kids/hurr.htm
The Federal Emergency Management Agency (FEMA) dedicates part of its kids' site to hurricanes.

www.noaa.gov/wx.html
The National Oceanic and Atmospheric Administration (NOAA) maintains a website with information on current and past weather events, weather alerts, and how to prepare for severe weather.

www.theweatherchannelkids.com
The Weather Channel's website just for kids provides information about different kinds of storms, weather games, short videos of cool weather events, and local forecasts.

www.weatherwizkids.com
This website is designed by a TV meteorologist. It explains weather conditions and storms. There is a glossary, weather jokes, and information for those interested in becoming a meteorologist.

INDEX